Let's Go

Written by Margie Burton, Cathy French, and Tammy Jones

He is going on the bus.

He is at school.

She is going
in the car.

She is at the store.

He is going
on a bike.

He is at the park.

He is at the station.

He is going on a train.

She is at the airport.

She is going on the plane.

She is at the lake.

She is going
on the boat.

He is at the barn.

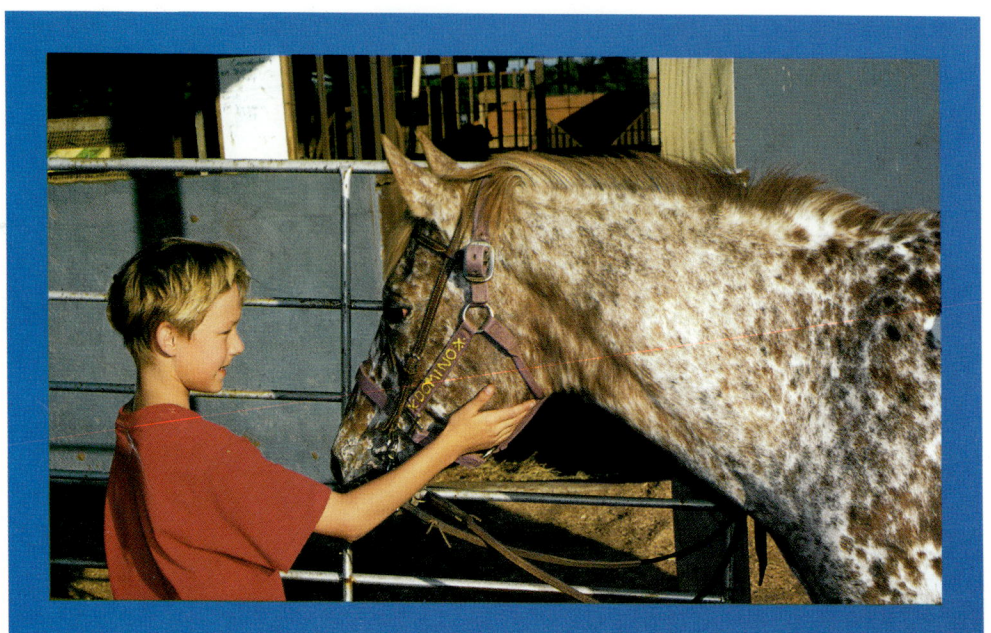

He is going
on a horse.

I am going to school.